The Surname Dutton

Susan Morris &
Wendy Bosberry-Scott

ISBN: 10: 153972350X
ISBN-13: 978-1539723509

The question of surnames, their origins, distribution and history, lies at the heart of genealogy as well as being fascinating in its own right.

In the 1980s and 1990s, long before many genealogical sources were even indexed, let alone online, our Surname Report service provided expert assessments of the origins, history and distribution of selected British surnames, using the sources available at the time.

Now, with so many more sources available, we believe that these reports retain their value as studies of individual surnames, and so we are gradually making the Debrett Surname Archive available online and in print for the first time. Some modern indexes have been consulted to refresh and update the reports.

Debrett Ancestry Research Ltd, PO Box 379,
Winchester SO23 9YQ
Tel: 01962 841904
Email: info@debrettancestry.co.uk
Website: www.debrettancestry.co.uk

CONTENTS

Overview

The use of surnames in England began in the Norman period, when surnames were not necessarily hereditary but usually a form of description. Some described the individual's trade or profession; others were nicknames; some gave the father's Christian name; others gave the individual's place of residence or origin.

Different surnames might be used in different documents, or more than one surname given in one document. Early descriptions were fairly elaborate and by the thirteenth and fourteenth centuries these were simpler, but still variable, and indeed the instability of surnames continued until well into the seventeenth century.

Although some Normans would already have had hereditary surnames on their arrival in Britain, the passing on of a surname from generation to generation only became customary in Britain gradually during the course of the thirteenth and fourteenth centuries. At the end of this period most of the population apparently had surnames.

Variations in the spelling of a family's surname continue to be found until the present century. Before this, as most people could not read or write, the parish clerk or other official would write down the name as they heard it.

There are four main groups of surnames:

A – Local names, which describe a person by his place of residence or origin.

B – Occupational names, which describe a person by his trade or profession.

C – Surnames of relationship, which refer to the Christian name of the father or other important relative.

D – Nicknames or sobriquets, coined to describe a person in terms of his appearance or character.

Many surnames have uncertain origins, but the name Dutton clearly falls into Category A.

Origins and early examples

There is a township of Dutton in the parish of Ribchester, Lancashire, six miles north of Blackburn. The place-name itself is derived from the Old English 'Dudda's Tun' (the homestead of Dudda's people), and appears as Duntun in the Domesday Book in 1086; it was already Dutton by 1288. Bardsley, the eminent Victorian authority on Anglo-American surnames, remarks that 'a family of Duttons arose here very early, and their ramifications have spread over the whole of Lancashire and the West Riding of Yorkshire'.

There was another township of Dutton, although smaller, across the border to the south in Cheshire, within the parish of Great Budworth. This Cheshire Dutton evidently gave rise to other holders of the surname, including one ancient family who, according to Ormerod's *History of Cheshire*, were:

> ...associated with that township form the time of William the Conqueror to the reign of Charles II...

This family is traditionally said to have been of Norman descent from Rollo, the conqueror of Neustria, through William Earl of Eu, who married a niece of William the Conqueror. The founder of the English branch is said to be Odard, kinsman of the famous Hugh Lupus, Earl of Chester, who gave him the barony of Dutton. There would have been other bearers of the surname, not connected with this manorial family, who were identified by the place-name when they moved to other parts of the country.

On the Cheshire/Denbighshire border, in Wales there are also Dutton Cacca, Dutton Diffeth and Dutton-y-Bran, all small hamlets. Early examples of the surname are as follows:

1332   Henry de Dutton of Bispham, Lancashire Lay Subsidy Roll

1414   John Dutton, citizen and tailor of London, probate

1415   William Dutton, Preston, Lancashire Guild Rolls

1428   Robert Dutton, citizen and saddler of London, probate

1579   Thomas Dutton, licensed to marry Judith Jennings in London

1594   Edmund Dutton, witness to deed relating to land at Parham, Suffolk

From the above it will be seen that the surname became established by immigration in London at an early date. By the time of the 1695 taxation census of London 'within the walls' there were five Dutton individuals as well as a family who lived in the parish of St Mary Magdalen, Old Fish Street.

Distribution

In 1890 H B Guppy published his *Homes of Family Names in Great Britain*, which is still the only published work on surname distribution in Britain as a whole. His work was based on printed genealogies and a survey of county directories for the 1880s, in which he looked especially at the names of farmers, reasoning that they were among the most stable groups in society. He restricted his study to names that appeared in a proportion of 7:10,000 or higher.

Guppy found that the surname Dutton occurred primarily in Cheshire (39:10,000) stating that:

> The Duttons of Dutton were a very old and distinguished family, and were associated with the township of that name from the time of William the Conqueror to the reign of Charles II. John and Rowland Dutton, evidently of this family, were two Cheshire gentlemen who contributed £25 a piece to the Spanish Armada fund in 1588.

The *English Surname Series*, which is very incomplete, shows that the surname Dutton appeared in Almondsbury in the West Riding of Yorkshire in the thirteenth century:

> 1258   Geoffrey de Dutton (Marsden) Steward

George Redmond, the author of this volume, suggested that the most likely explanation for the appearance of a Lancashire surname in Yorkshire at this date:

… seems to be that there had been some movement of tenants between manors, owing to the way in which the larger landholders had manors in various parts of the country. The fact that much land in this area had belonged to the Earls of Lancaster would explain the frequency of the Lancashire surnames.

In H R Moulton's *Palaeography, Genealogy and Topography*, primarily a sale catalogue printed in 1930 listing historical documents, ancient charters, leases, court rolls *etc.*, there were two entries for the name Dutton:

27 January 1590

Three membranes. Deed of Settlement. Besthorpe, Norfolk. Hon Robert Paston of St Martin in the Fields, and Anne his wife of 1st part. Sir Richard Dutton of St Martin in the Fields, Thomas Doughty of St Paul's Covent Garden, of 2nd part. Hon Thomas Paston of St James Middlesex, Hon Roger North of Middle Temple of 3rd part. Hon William Earl of Yarmouth, John Herbert of Gunton, county Norfolk, John Ayde of Horsted, Co Norfolk of 4th part
Witnesses: Jo Warkhouse, John King, Henry Cranston, Fran Cruso
Signatures of all parties, 7 seals £2 2/-

9 February 1594

Grant by Thomas Cosyn of Melton, County Suffolk, yeoman to John Bill, clerk, vicar of Sutton, county Suffolk, of two pieces of land in Parham, County Suffolk, containing one acre, of which one piece lies between the bond tenement, late of the said Thomas Cosyn and the meadow of William Bardwell, and abuts on the highway from Framlingham to Woodbridge on the west and the common stream on the east and the other piece called Shepperdes yarde lies between bond land of the Manor of Parham late in the tenure of William Goodinge on the south, and land late of John Pearse on the north and abuts on the said stream on the east and the highway from Framlingham to Parham on the west, which premises the grantor lately had of the gift of John Cosyn, son and next heir of Robert Cosyn late of Parham deceased, by charter dated 24 September, 4 Elizabeth, 9 February 30 Elizabeth.

Witnesses: Edmund Dutton, Charles Bardwell, Robert Mershe, Geoffrey Haughfyn.   £2

The surname Dutton was thus found in Norfolk and Suffolk in the sixteenth century. A check of McKinley's *Norfolk Surnames in the Sixteenth Century* found no mention of the name Dutton, suggesting perhaps that its appearance in the sixteenth century deeds was for men who were not native to East Anglia.

George F Black's authoritative dictionary of *The Surnames of Scotland* does not list the surname Dutton. Nor was any entry found for the surname in McKinley's *A History of British Surnames*, Cottle's *Surnames*, Reaney's *The Origin of English Surnames* or Lasker and Mascie-Taylor's *Atlas of British Surnames*. The latter work showing a negative result was somewhat surprising in that Lasker and Mascie-Taylor used, as one of their sources, Guppy's work, which we have discussed above. Reaney's *Dictionary of English Surnames* (revised by R M Wilson, 3rd edition) deals with Dutton as follows:

> **Dutton**
> c1150   Richard de Duttona, *The Staffordshire Chartulary* (Salt Arch Society (OS) 2, 3, 1881, 1882)
> 1246   Richard de Dutton, Lancashire Assizes

1468   John Dutton, *Inquisitiones Post Mortem,*
            Nottinghamshire
        From Dutton, Cheshire and Lancashire

Dutton was found in Staffordshire in the mid-twelfth century as de Duttona. In the mid-thirteenth century Richard de Dutton's name appears in the assizes records for Lancashire and in the fifteenth century, Reaney found a John Dutton in Nottinghamshire. He stated that he believed the name to derive from the place-name Dutton of Cheshire and Lancashire.

J J Kneen, in his work, *Manx Personal Names*, mentions Dutton thus:

> **Dutton** (local name from estates, villages or towns)
> Dutton (Bridge House (Castletown, Mann) Collection) 1490
> 'of Dutton' (Cheshire place-name)
> Peeres Dutton, 'Esquier', was one of the Earl of Derby's chaplains in 1490

Kneen found one entry for the name in a collection of documents for Castletown from the fifteenth century. He states, however, that the name is not a local one and that Piers Dutton was a chaplain for the Earl of Derby, presumably holding one of the Earl's livings on Man.

Many of the sources available for charting surname distribution through the centuries are necessarily confined to the wealthier sectors of the population: in general, nobody wanted to know the names of the poor but the names of those with money or land were naturally of interest to the authorities. However, one source that covers the whole of the social spectrum is provided by English parish registers, the earliest of which began in 1538 following a mandate that all parish priests should keep a weekly record of all baptisms, marriages and burials that took place in their parish. A survey of a cross section of parish registers for the years 1601 and 1602 was carried out in 1910 by F K and S Hitching; incidences of a particular surname are noted by parish and county, although with no indication of numbers of references.

In 1601 the name Dutton was found in the parish registers of Gloucestershire, Lancashire and London.

A useful guide to the distribution of surnames for the sixteenth, seventeenth and eighteenth centuries in England is provided by the indexes to wills proved, and administrations granted, at the Prerogative Court of (the Archbishop of) Canterbury, in London, which had superior jurisdiction over local ecclesiastical courts where wills were proved until 1858. The PCC thus provides a national index, although it is not a completely representative one, as testators whose wills were proved in the PCC were mostly among the wealthier members of society, and a disproportionate number of them were from London or Middlesex.

A search of the indexes for the years 1584 to 1857 found numerous entries for people named Dutton from all over England and can be summarised as follows:

1558-1599
1581   Thomas Dutton esq, Sherborn, Northleach, Gloucestershire
1582   Margaret Dutton, afterwards Coton; former husband Thomas Dutton, Sherborne, Gloucestershire

1585   John Dutton, gentleman, servant
1586   Hughe Dutton
1594   Thomas Dutton, gentleman of Isleworth, Middx

Seventeenth Century

1615   Thomas Dutton of Turkdean, Gloucestershire
1617   William Dutton, haberdasher of London
1618   William Dutton of Sherborne, Gloucestershire
1623   George Dutton, brewer of London
1623   Joan Dutton, widow of Isleworth London
1634   Thomas Dutton, servant of Enfield, Middx
1639   Peter Dutton of Hooton, Cheshire
1640   Lord Gerrard, Baron Dutton of Eccleshall, Staffordshire
1641   Thomas Dutton, gentleman of Winshill, Derbyshire
1642   Roger Dutton, salter of London
1650   George Dutton
1651   Anne Dutton, widow of Sherborne, Gloucestershire
1653   John Dutton, yeoman, Perry Barre (Handsworth), Staffordshire
1655   Peeter Dutton, husbandman, Cuddington, Cheshire
1657   Ellnor Dutton, widow, Downton, Wiltshire
1657   John Dutton esq, Sherborne, Gloucestershire
1657   William Dutton senior, Downton, Wiltshire
1658   Edmond Dutton, yeoman, Chinnor, Oxfordshire
1661   James Dugdale or Dutton, vicar of Evercreech and rector of Shepton, Beauchamp, doctor of theology of Evercreech, Somerset
1669   Anne Dutton, spinster, late of London now of Stoke Newington, Middlesex
1673   Phillipp Dutton, gentleman of Abington, Berkshire
1676   William Dutton of Sherborne, Gloucestershire

1681 John Dutton, gentleman of Newington, Oxon
1684 Susanna Dutton, widow of London
1690 Mary Dutton, widow of St Andrew Holborn,
      Middx
1693 Henry Dutton, clerk, rector of Mells, Somerset
1697 Judith Dutton, widow of All Hallows Barking,
      London
1698 John Dutton, upholster of St Sepulchre, Middx
1699 John Dutton, gentleman of St Giles
      Cripplegate, London
1699 Elizabeth Dutton, widow of St Martin in the
      Fields, Middx

Eighteenth Century

1702 John Dutton, gentleman of Burton,
      Staffordshire
1704 Sir Richard Dutton
1707 Samuel Dutton, tobacconist of Framsden,
      Suffolk
1715 Joshua Dutton, gentleman of New Castle,
      Staffordshire
1717 Leonard Dutton, yeoman of Chinnor, Oxon
1717 Ralph Dutton of Sherborne, Gloucestershire
1719 Bartholomew Dutton, gentleman of Middle
      Temple, City of London
1721 Sir Ralph Dutton of Rathfernam, County
      Dublin
1721 Laurence Dutton, mariner now belonging to
      HMS Ipswich
1721 Mary Dutton, widow of St Clement Danes,
      Middx
1723 Richard Dutton, currier of Greenwich, Kent
1723 Dame Mary Dutton, widow of St Martin in the
      Fields, Middx
1726 Honoria Dutton, widow of St Clement Danes,
      Middx
1728 Elizabeth Dutton, widow of Little Distaffe
      Lane, Old Fish Street, City of London

1732   John Dutton, yeoman of Cookham, Berkshire
1732   Ann Dutton, widow of Cookham, Berkshire
1732   Henry Neale Dutton of Windsor, Berkshire
1733   Ann Dutton, spinster of St Martins in the
       Fields, Middx
1735   John Dutton, distiller of Shrewsbury,
       Shropshire
1736   Hugh Dutton, sedan maker of St Giles in the
       Fields, Middx
1740   Henry Dutton of St Bartholomew the Less,
       City of London
1743   Sir John Dutton of Sherborne, Gloucestershire
1746   Leonard Dutton, yeoman of Cookham,
       Berkshire
1749   Mark Dutton, gentleman of Ebbisham, Surrey
1751   John Dutton, tobacconist of St Botolph without
       Aldgate, Middx
1751   Adam Dutton, gentleman of St Dunstan
       Stepney, Middx
1752   Samuel Dutton now belonging to HMS Prince
1752   Elizabeth Dutton, widow of St Georges
       Bloomsbury, Middx
1753   Daniel Dutton, victualler of St George the
       Martyr, Surrey
1754   John Dutton, baker of Hampstead, Middx
1754   John Dutton, mealman of Maidenhead,
       Berkshire
1756   John Dutton of City of London
1757   Joseph Dutton of St Dunstan in the West, City
       of London
1758   Samuel Dutton of Council at Fort
       Marlborough on the west coast of Sumatra in
       service of the Honourable English East India
       Company
1760   Hester Dutton, widow of Houndsditch, City of
       London
1760   Mary Dutton, widow of Shrewsbury,
       Shropshire

1762 Mary Dutton, widow of Cookham, Berkshire

1762 Jemima Dutton, spinster of Sherborne, Gloucestershire

1762 John Dutton, bricklayer of St Martin in the Fields, Middx

1763 Eve Dutton, widow of St Mary Whitechapel, Middx

1763 Rev Matthew Dutton, rector of Hinderwell, Yorkshire

1763 Elizabeth Dutton, spinster of Newport, Shropshire

1764 Joseph Dutton, mariner now of HMS Dreadnought

1765 Matthew Dutton, gentleman of Steppingley, Bedfordshire

1768 Peter Dutton, gentleman of Bunhill Row, London

1770 John Dutton, butcher of Enfield, Middx

1771 John Lenox Dutton of Maidenhead Thicket, Berkshire

1771 Esan Dutton, butcher of Edmonton, Middx

1772 John Dutton, gentleman of Beckbury, Shropshire

1773 Henry Dutton, taylor of Loughborough, Leicestershire

1773 Matthew Dutton, shipwright of Poplar, Middx

1774 Richard Dutton, grocer of St Margaret Westminster, Middx

1777 Benjamin Dutton, hat maker of St Peter Westcheap

1777 Edward Dutton of Whitechapel, Middx

1777 James Lenox Dutton of Sherborne, Gloucestershire

1778 John Dutton of Wantage, Berkshire

1779 William Dutton, gentleman of St Ann Westminster, Middx

1780 Moses Dutton, porter of St Luke Old Street, Middx

1782	Samuel Dutton, gentleman of St George Hanover Sq, Middx
1782	Elizabeth Dutton, widow of Golden Lane, near Old Street, Middx
1783	Thomas Dutton, boatswain of HMS Adamant
1784	Thomas Dutton of St Mary Whitechapel, Middx
1785	James Dutton, house steward of Romsey Extra, Hampshire
1786	William Dutton, gentleman of Harborne, Staffordshire
1786	Benjamin Dutton of St Ann Westminster, Middx
1789	Mary Dutton, widow of Bond Street, St George Hanover Sq, Middx
1791	Susannah Dutton, widow of St Dunstan Stepney, Middx
1791	Edward Dutton, cheesemonger of Gt Portland Street, Middx
1794	Joseph Dutton of Little Marlow, Buckinghamshire
1794	William Dutton watchmaker of St Dunstan in the West, City of London
1796	Richard Dutton, boatswain of HM Dock Yard of Plymouth, Devon
1796	Michael Dutton, Master at Arms (No 266) late belonging to the ship Impregnable but now of the Ship Royal William, Master at Arms (No 2207183) of Portsmouth, Hampshire
1798	Richard Dutton, midshipman now belonging to HMS Orion
1799	Elizabeth Dutton, widow of Coddington, Cheshire
1799	Elizabeth Dutton

It will be noted that several of these probates are for testators in the south-western counties of Gloucestershire and Wiltshire, while none is for a

Lancashire testator; however, as stated, the PCC does show a bias towards the southern counties (the Prerogative Court of York would show more Lancashire entries). It will be remembered that Gloucestershire was one of the counties picked out by the 1601 and 1602 surveys of parish registers as having Dutton references; and the IGI, an index of baptisms and marriages compiled in the main from parish registers, shows the name Dutton to be very substantially represented in Gloucestershire. References can be seen to the name in Sherborne (and other parishes) from the sixteenth century to the nineteenth.

The reason for this Gloucestershire concentration of Duttons lies with the ancient and prolific family of Dutton from Cheshire. In the sixteenth century Thomas Dutton esquire purchased the manor of Sherborne from Sir Christopher Alleyn. The Alleyn family were resident in Kent at this time and while Burke states that it was the manor of Sherborne, Dorset, which was purchased, this is probably an error. Thomas died in 1581 and it is evidently his will that was proved at the PCC in that year. His son William became Sheriff of Gloucester and had seven sons and seven daughters. The eldest son, John, was one of the knights who sat in parliament in 1640 but, being a Royalist, retreated to Oxford, where he was influential in defending the city against the parliamentarians. He was described as:

> ... a learned and prudent man, and as one of the richest, so one of the meekest men in England

The Duttons of Sherborne continued in public service and Ralph Dutton MP was created a Baronet by Charles II in 1678. The baronetcy became in extinct in 1743, but the estates passed to the related Naper family, who changed their name to Dutton. James Dutton, who inherited the English estates of the family, was elevated to the peerage as Baron Sherborn in 1784. The Barons Sherborne retained their allegiance to Oxford and owned Windrush Manor, near Burford, there until the twentieth century as well as Sherborne Park. Another branch of the family settled at Hinton Ampner in Hampshire.

Returning to the eighteenth century, and the PCC indexes, the picture is more diffuse. Discounting entries for London, Middlesex and Surrey, and for those who died abroad or at sea, entries were found for Cheshire, Shropshire, Leicestershire and Staffordshire in the mid-west; for Gloucestershire, Somerset and Devon in the south-west; and for Hampshire, Berkshire, Oxfordshire, Buckinghamshire, Bedfordshire and Kent in the south-east. Even taking into account the bias of the PCC it is notable that there is not a single entry for Lancashire but there is one for Yorkshire and we have the will of Sir Ralph Dutton of Dublin in 1721.

In the nineteenth century we found 80 Dutton entries in the PCC indexes, as follows:

1800-1857

1802   Richard Dutton, gentleman of Hethe, Oxfordshire
1803   Thomas Dutton, gentleman of Shire Lane, Temple Bar, Middx
1804   Ralph Dutton of Billingford, Norfolk
1807   Honoria Dutton, widow of Bath, Somerset
1809   Richard Dutton of Twickenham, Kent

1811 Margaret otherwise Margret Dutton, widow of Birmingham, Warwickshire

1812 Mary Dutton, wife of Warrington, Lancashire

1813 Richard Dutton, of St Leonard Shoreditch, Middx

1814 Cornelius Dutton, brickmaker of St Nicholas, Warwickshire

1815 John Dutton of Kennington Road, Surrey

1816 Thomas Dutton, gentleman of Birmingham, Warwickshire

1816 Joseph Dutton, gentleman of Birmingham, Warwickshire

1818 Mary Dutton, widow of Princes Square, Kennington, Surrey

1819 Mary Dutton, spinster of Wolverhampton, Staffordshire

1820 Joseph Dutton, agent to Worthington & Co of Birmingham, Warwickshire

1820 Mary Dutton, widow of Handsworth, Staffordshire

1821 Peter Dutton of St Martin's Place, Chester, Cheshire

1822 Abigail Dutton, widow of Brackley, Northamptonshire

1822 John Dutton, Linen Merchant of Chester, Cheshire

1822 Thomas Dutton, gentleman of Thornton, Cheshire

1823 Mary Dutton, widow of Hoxton Square, Middx

1823 Sarah Dutton, widow of Whitchurch, Shropshire

1823 Sarah Dutton, spinster of Twickenham, Middx

1824 Sarah Golden otherwise Golding formerly Dutton, widow of Stepney, Middx

1825 Samuel Dutton, gentleman of Broxton, Cheshire

1825	Anne Dutton otherwise Ann Hutchinson of Basinghall Street, City of London
1825	Phebe Dutton late Phebe Dixon, wife of Horsely House, Staffordshire
1826	Ann Dutton, spinster of Devonshire St, Vauxhall, Surrey
1826	Hannah Felicia Dutton, spinster of Richmond, Surrey
1830	Sarah Dutton, widow of Twickenham, Middx
1830	Frederick Dutton, gentleman of 32 Holborn, near Grays Inn Gate, Middx
1831	Richard Dutton, gentleman of Mickleton, Gloucestershire
1831	William Dutton, gentleman of Eastbourne, Sussex
1832	Mary Dutton, spinster of Tattenhall, Cheshire
1833	Mary Dutton or Spiegel, wife of Chesterfield, Derbyshire
1834	Ann Dutton, widow of Stanthorne Hall, Cheshire
1835	John Dutton of Stokenchurch, Oxfordshire
1836	Joshua Dutton of Portsmouth, Hampshire
1838	John Vaughan Dutton of Bruton Street, Bond Street, Middx
1838	Thomas Dutton, Commander in the Royal Navy of Southsea, Portsmouth, Hampshire
1838	James Dutton, scalemaker of St Giles Camberwell, Surrey
1838	John Dutton of St Martin Birmingham, Warwickshire
1839	Charles Dutton of Hilmorton, Warwickshire
1839	Joseph Dutton of Pinner, Middx
1839	Mary Dutton, spinster of Stokenchurch, Oxfordshire
1839	Anne or Ann Dutton, spinster formerly servant of Windsor, Berkshire
1840	Elizabeth Dutton, spinster of Chester, Cheshire

1842   Alfred Newman Dutton, clerk in HM Customs of 15 Duncan Terrace, Islington, Middx

1842   John Dutton, gentleman of Madeley, Shropshire

1843   Mary Dutton, spinster of Kings Langley, Hertfordshire

1843   Mary Dutton, widow of Acton, Cheshire

1844   Thomas Dutton, wholesale stationer of Thames Street, City of London

1844   William Dutton, builder of Atherstone, Warwickshire

1845   Elizabeth Dutton, spinster of Stokenchurch, Oxfordshire

1847   George Dutton, gentleman of Camberwell, Surrey

1848   Frederick Hugh Hampden Dutton, HM Post Office Agent of Rotterdam, Netherlands

1848   John Dutton, gentleman of Southampton, Hampshire

1849   Thomas Dutton, gentleman of Tattenhall, Cheshire

1849   William Dutton, gentleman of Halewood House, Lancashire

1849   Henry Dutton, grocer of 84 Whitecross Street, Middx

1849   Thomas Dutton of Claines, Worcestershire

1850   George Dutton, farmer of Coddington, Cheshire

1850   Matthew Dutton, watchmaker of Stoke Newington, Middx

1850   Thomas Holland Mason Dutton, chemist of Bath, Somerset

1851   Jesse Dutton, surgeon of Stokenchurch, Oxfordshire

1851   John Dutton, stonemason or bricklayer of Cheadle, Staffordshire

1852   Elizabeth Dutton of Netherton, Worcestershire

1852   Eliza Dutton, spinster of Brixton Rise, Surrey

1852   Catharine Dutton, widow of Birkenhead,
        Cheshire
1853   James Sutton, surgeon of St Clements, Sussex
1853   Sophia Augusta Dutton, spinster of Islington,
        Middx
1853   Benjamin Dutton, Commander in HM Navy of
        Hastings, Sussex
1854   Catherine Dutton, widow of Crewe near
        Farndon, Cheshire
1855   Mary Dutton, widow of Hastings, Sussex
1856   Joseph Dutton, gentleman of York, Yorkshire
1856   Robert William Dutton, watchmaker of Fleet
        Street, City of London
1856   Douglas Dutton, surgeon of 73 Connaught
        Terrace, Edgeware Road, Middx
1857   Mary Ann Dutton, spinster of Chesterfield,
        Derbyshire
1857   Samuel Dutton, gentleman of Chesterfield,
        Derbyshire
1857   Hugh Cawley Dutton, farmer of Bunbury,
        Cheshire

As can be seen, the surname was now widespread across most of England with many entries for Cheshire and Lancashire and one for a testator who died in Holland in 1848.

H B Guppy's survey has been mentioned above. Another important Victorian source is the *Return of Owners of Land of 1873*, sometimes known as the Modern Domesday Book. This source lists, county by county, every owner of an acre of land or more, with their residence (not necessarily the address of their property) and the acreage of their holding. Guppy mentions the Duttons of Dutton in Cheshire, and notes that John and Rowland Dutton were two Cheshire gentlemen who contributed £25 each to the Spanish Armada fund in 1588. In Victorian times Guppy writes that the Duttons 'are now numerous in the Nantwich district'. Cheshire was the only county picked out by Guppy's study of directories as having a notable concentration of Dutton entries.

Thus Bardsley's remark that a family of Duttons arose in Lancashire 'very early', with 'ramifications spread over the whole of Lancashire and the West Riding of Yorkshire', needs to be qualified. There certainly were Duttons in Lancashire from the fourteenth century, as shown above, but nationally the Cheshire Duttons have had the greater influence. The IGI for Lancashire shows a good number of Duttons, but most of these are from the eighteenth century onwards, and the proportion to the county as a whole is not large.

Return of Owners of Land

Berkshire 1
Cheshire 13
Derbyshire 3
Gloucestershire 4
Hampshire 3
Herefordshire 1
Kent 1
Lancashire 8
Leicestershire and Rutland 1
Middlesex 1
Oxfordshire 4
Shropshire 2
Somerset 1
Staffordshire 3
Yorkshire, West Riding 2

Landowners with the name Dutton owned land in across all of England with higher concentrations of the name appearing, as expected, in Cheshire and Lancashire.

Famous bearers of the name

In Debrett's *People of Today* (1996), the following references to people with the name Dutton were found:

> Major General Bryan Hawkins Dutton, CBE, OBE, MBE
> Richard Odard Astley Dutton (of Dutton family of Sherborne, Gloucestershire)
> Timothy James Dutton, lawyer

Another Tim Dutton, an actor born in Warwickshire, is known for his work on programmes such as *Midsomer Murders*, *Lewis* and *Pie in the Sky* as well as parts in films such as *Patriot Games* and *The Bourne Identity*.

Ralph Dutton (1898-1985) was the 8th and last Baron Sherborne, who gifted Hinton Ampner manor in Hampshire to the National Trust upon his death; his book *Hinton Ampner: A Hampshire Manor* (1969) is an account of the families who owned the manor.

There are eleven coats of arms listed in Burke's *General Armory* granted to men of the name Dutton:

> Dutton of Dutton, Cheshire
> Dutton of Hatton, Cheshire
> Dutton, bart of Sherborne, Dorset [sic] extinct 1743
> Dutton, Baron Sherborn
> Dutton, granted 1647 to Lt Richard Dutton (Irish)
> Dutton of Cheshire
> Dutton of Cheshire
> Dutton (no location given)
> Dutton of Bulkley and Cheadle, Cheshire

Dutton (William De Dutton) Cheshire
Dutton, granted to Frederick Hansbrow Dutton of
Piccadilly and Australia

Printed Genealogies

The following references have been found for families named Dutton:

Memorials of the Duttons of Dutton (London and Chester), 1891, 4to.

Samuel Rudder, *The Histories and Antiquities of Gloucestershire*, 649.

G W Marshall, *Collections for a Genealogical Account of the Family of Comberbach*, (London, 1866), 55.

Burke's *Landed Gentry*, 3rd edition, 4th edition, 1937, 1972 editions.

Joseph Foster, *Visitations of Yorkshire 1563-4*, 241.

Burke's *Royal Descents and Pedigrees of Founders' Kin*, 48.

George Ormerod, *The History of the County Palatine and City of Chester 1785-1873*, I, 643; ii, 795; iii, 622.

T D Fosbrooke, *Original History of the city of Gloucester*, ii, 388.

Edmondson's *Baronagium Genealogicum*, vi, 123.

Sir Egerton Brydges, *Collins' Peerage of England* (1812), viii, 39.

Thomas Wotton, *The Baronetage of England*, iii, 642.

Burke's *Extinct & Dormant Baronetcies.*

Chetham Society, cx, 223.

Harleian Society, xviii, 87, 237, 260; xxi, 53, 54; xxxix, 1013, 1018.

Visitations of Gloucester, edited by T F Fenwich & W C Metcalfe, 19.

Burke's *Colonial Gentry,* ii, 529.

The Genealogist, New Series, xii, 112; xiii, 99.

Visitations of Cheshire 1613

Harleian Society, lix, 90, 92

Middlesex Pedigrees (Harleian Society) lxv, 103.

Miscellanea Genealogica et Heraldica, 4th Series, v, 289.

F A Crisp, *Visitations of England and Wales,* x, 20

Ruvigny, *The Plantagenet Roll of the Blood Royal: The Clarence Volume* (1905) 623.

William Salt Society, *Collections for a History of Staffordshire, New Series,* xii, 248.

Transactions of the Lancashire and Cheshire Antiquarian Society, ii, 233.

Pedigrees of the Family of James of Culgarth, West Auckland, and Barrock and their Kinsfolk (1913, 1914), 7.

H L L Denny, *Memorials of an Ancient House: A History of the Family of Lister or Lyster* (1913), 9.

V J Watney, *The Wallop Family and Their Ancestry* (1928), pg291.

T H D Colley, *The Family of Colley of Churton Heath in the County of Chester* (1931)

G Cope, *Genealogy of the Dutton Family of Pennsylvania, preceded by a History of the Family in England*, (West Chester, PA, 1871)

Burke's *Peerage & Baronetage* (1970)

Burke's *Authorised Arms*

Summary

To conclude, the name Dutton derives from the Lancashire place-name and has spread to all parts of England but remains most concentrated in Lancashire, Cheshire and Gloucestershire.

Sources Consulted

P H Reaney, *The Origins of English Surnames* (London: Routledge & Kegan Paul 1967)

P H Reaney & R M Wilson, *Dictionary of British Surnames* (London: Oxford University Press, 3rd edition 1995)

P H Reaney, *Dictionary of British Surnames* (London: Routledge & Kegan Paul, 2nd edition 1976)

P Hanks & F Hodges, *A Dictionary of Surnames* (Oxford University Press 1988)

M A Lower, *Patronymica Brittanica* (London 1860)

C W Bardsley, *Dictionary of English and Welsh Surnames* (1901: reprinted, Baltimore: Genealogical Publishing Co. 1967)

C L'Estrange Ewen, *Guide to the Origin of British Surnames* (London: John Gifford 1938)

H B Guppy, *Homes of Family Names in Great Britain* (London 1890)

Ernest Weekley, *The Romance of Names* (London: John Murray, 2nd edition 1917)

Ernest Weekley, *Surnames* (London: John Murray 1917)

George F Black, *The Surnames of Scotland* (New York Public Library 1946)

Edward McLysaght, *The Surnames of Ireland* (Dublin: Irish University Press 1977)

T J & Prys Morgan, *Welsh Surnames* (Cardiff: University of Wales Press 1985)

J J Kneen, *Manx Personal Names* (Oxford, 1937)

F K & S Hitching, *References to English Surnames in 1601* (Walton on Thames: Bernau 1910)

F K & S Hitching, *References to English Surnames in 1602* (Walton on Thames: Bernau 1911)

Basil Cottle, *The Penguin Dictionary of Surnames* (Allen Lane, 1978)

R A McKinley, *A History of British Surnames* (Longman, 1995)

G W Lasker & C G N Mascie-Taylor, *Atlas of British Surnames* (Detroit, 1990)

Debrett's *People of Today* (Debrett's Peerage Limited 1996)

The Dictionary of National Biography: Index & Epitome (London 1906)

The Concise Dictionary of National Biography, Part II, 1901-1950, (Oxford 1961)

Burke's *Family Index* (London: Burke's Peerage Limited 1976)

H R Moulton, *Palaeography, Genealogy & Topography* (1930)

Prerogative Court of Canterbury Wills (online index)

Online index to England, Scotland and Wales census returns 1841-1911

G W Marshall, *The Genealogist's Guide* (1903; reprinted, Baltimore: GPC 1973)

J B Whitmore, *A Genealogical Guide* (London 1953)

Charles Bridge, *An Index to Pedigrees* (London 1867)

Geoffrey B Barrow, *The Genealogist's Guide* (London: Research Publishing Co. 1977)

Sir Bernard Burke, *The General Armory* (London 1884)

C R Humphrey-Smith, ed, *Burke's General Armory Volume II*, (Tabard Press 1973)

The Return of Owners of Land (1873)

Eilert Ekwall, *The Oxford Dictionary of English Place-Names*

E G Withycombe, *The Oxford Dictionary of English Christian Names* (Oxford: Clarendon Press, 2nd edition 1950)

W J Hardy & W Page, *A Calendar to the Feet of Fines for London and Middlesex: Vol 1 Richard I- Richard III (1189-1485)* (London 1892)

Richard McKinley, *The Surnames of Oxford*, (Leopards Head Press, 1977)

Richard McKinley, *The Surnames of Sussex*, (Leopards Head Press, 1988)

Richard McKinley, *The Surnames of Lancashire*, (Leopards Head Press, 1981)

Richard McKinley, *The Surnames of Norfolk and Suffolk*, (Phillimore 1975)

R A McKinley, *Norfolk Surnames in the Sixteenth Century* (Leicester, 1969)

George Redmonds, *The Surnames of Yorkshire West Riding*, (Phillimore 1973)

Mr Avenell, *The Norman People*, (London 1874)

Debrett's *Heraldry*, (London 1933)

Boutell's *Heraldry* (Warne, 1970)